OCT 25 2005

S0-BCO-844

IMMIGRANT KIDS

Children's rooftop playground at Ellis Island. Children
could stay here while their parents were being questioned
and examined. (photo by Augustus F. Sherman)

IMMIGRANT KIDS

by Russell Freedman

Macedon Public Library
30 Main St.
Macedon, NY 14502

PUFFIN BOOKS

PUFFIN BOOKS
Published by the Penguin Group
Penguin Putnam Books for Young Readers,
345 Hudson Street, New York, New York 10014, U.S.A.
Penguin Books Ltd, 80 Strand, London WC2R ORL, England
Penguin Books Australia Ltd, Ringwood, Victoria, Australia
Penguin Books Canada Ltd, 10 Alcorn Avenue, Toronto, Ontario, Canada M4V 3B2
Penguin Books (N.Z.) Ltd, 182-190 Wairau Road, Auckland 10, New Zealand
Penguin Books Ltd, Registered Offices: Harmondsworth, Middlesex, England

First published in the United States of America by E. P. Dutton, 1980
Published in Puffin Books, 1995

19   20

Copyright © Russell Freedman, 1980
All rights reserved

THE LIBRARY OF CONGRESS HAS CATALOGED THE DUTTON EDITION AS FOLLOWS:
Freedman, Russell.
Immigrant kids.
Includes index.
Summary: Text and period photographs chronicle the life of immigrant
children at home, school, work, and play during the late 1800s and early 1900s.
1. Children of immigrants—United States—Juvenile literature.
[1. United States—Emigration and immigration. 2. City and town life.]   I. Title.
HQ796.F7635   301.43'14   79-20060   ISBN 0-525-32538-7

Quotation permissions and photo sources are listed on page 69

Puffin Books ISBN 0-14-037594-5

Printed in the United States of America

Except in the United States of America, this book is sold subject to the condition that
it shall not, by way of trade or otherwise, be lent, re-sold, hired out, or otherwise
circulated without the publisher's prior consent in any form of binding or cover
other than that in which it is published and without a similar condition
including this condition being imposed on the subsequent purchaser.

to my grandparents

Contents

Preface

The boys and girls in these old photographs were born nearly a century ago. They grew up during the late 1800s and early 1900s, when millions of immigrants arrived in the United States from every corner of Europe.

Some of the children shown here came to America with their parents. Others were the first in their families to be born on American soil. All of them lived in crowded immigrant neighborhoods of America's big cities around the turn of the century.

Photography was still a young, fast-growing science. Small, hand-held cameras appeared for the first time during the 1880s. They were called "detective cameras" because their owners could snap pictures quickly and easily without being observed. These new cameras led to the great age of the amateur photographer. Now anyone could take on-the-spot photos of ordinary people going about their daily lives.

Many of the photographs in this book were taken by Jacob A. Riis, a New York City newspaper reporter. Riis was an immigrant from Denmark. To record the lives of poor immigrants who were struggling to establish themselves in America, he learned to use a detective camera. Riis was one of the first photographers to take documentary flash-light photos inside tenements and sweatshops. Some of his early photos were printed in his famous book, *How the Other Half Lives*, published in 1890.

Another pioneering photographer whose pictures appear here was Lewis Hine, who took thousands of pictures of immigrants and working people. Hine devoted much of his life to a crusade against child labor. He proved that photographs could be a powerful force for social change. His graphic photos of young children at work—like the laundry worker on page 43—helped bring about reforms that made child labor illegal in the United States.

Some of the other pictures in this book were taken by unknown photographers. Their names have been lost to us, but the living images they captured with their cameras still exist today. We can look at these images and see immigrant children growing up long ago. We can catch a glimpse of the way they lived, learned, worked, and played.

Two immigrant kids (photo by Augustus F. Sherman)

Coming Over

In the years around the turn of the century, immigration to America reached an all-time high. Between 1880 and 1920, 23 million immigrants arrived in the United States. They came mainly from the countries of Europe, especially from impoverished towns and villages in southern and eastern Europe. The one thing they had in common was a fervent belief that in America, life would be better.

Most of these immigrants were poor. Somehow they managed to scrape together enough money to pay for their passage to America. Many immigrant families arrived penniless. Others had to make the journey in stages. Often the father came first, found work, and sent for his family later.

Immigrants usually crossed the Atlantic as steerage passengers. Reached by steep, slippery stairways, the steerage lay deep down in the hold of the ship. It was occupied by passengers paying the lowest fare.

Men, women, and children were packed into dark, foul-smelling compartments. They slept in narrow bunks stacked three high. They had no showers, no lounges, and no dining rooms. Food served from huge kettles was dished into dinner pails provided by the steamship company. Because steerage conditions were crowded and uncomfortable, passengers spent as much time as possible up on deck.

Steerage deck of the immigrant liner
S.S. Pennland, 1893 (photo by Byron)

The voyage was an ordeal, but it was worth it. They were on their way to America.

The great majority of immigrants landed in New York City, at America's busiest port. They never forgot their first glimpse of the Statue of Liberty.

Immigrants crowd the deck as the S.S. Patricia sails into New York harbor on December 10, 1906. (photo by Edwin Levick)

Edward Corsi, who later became United States Commissioner of Immigration, was a ten-year-old Italian immigrant when he sailed into New York harbor in 1907:

My first impressions of the New World will always remain etched in my memory, particularly that hazy October morning when I first saw Ellis Island. The steamer *Florida*, fourteen days out of Naples, filled to capacity with 1600 natives of Italy, had weathered one of the worst storms in our captain's memory; and glad we were, both children and grown-ups, to leave the open sea and come at last through the Narrows into the Bay.

My mother, my stepfather, my brother Giuseppe, and my two sisters, Liberta and Helvetia, all of us together, happy that we had come through the storm safely, clustered on the foredeck for fear of separation and looked with wonder on this miraculous land of our dreams.

Giuseppe and I held tightly to Stepfather's hands, while Liberta and Helvetia clung to Mother. Passengers all about us were crowding against the rail. Jabbered conversation, sharp cries, laughs and cheers —a steadily rising din filled the air. Mothers and fathers lifted up babies so that they too could see, off to the left, the Statue of Liberty....

Finally the *Florida* veered to the left, turning northward into the Hudson River, and now the incredible buildings of lower Manhattan came very close to us.

The officers of the ship...went striding up and down the decks shouting orders and directions and driving the immigrants before them. Scowling and gesturing, they pushed and pulled the passengers, herding us into separate groups as though we were animals. A few moments later we came to our dock, and the long journey was over.

New arrivals

But the journey was not yet over. Before they could be admitted to the United States, immigrants had to pass through Ellis Island, which became the nation's chief immigrant processing center in 1892. There they would be questioned and examined. Those who could not pass all the exams would be detained; some would be sent back to Europe. And so their arrival in America was filled with great anxiety. Among the immigrants, Ellis Island was known as "Heartbreak Island."

When their ship docked at a Hudson River pier, the immigrants had numbered identity tags pinned to their clothing. Then they were herded onto special ferryboats that carried them to Ellis Island. Officials hurried them along, shouting "Quick! Run! Hurry!" in half a dozen languages.

Some immigrants had big families.
(photo by Augustus F. Sherman)

The great inspection hall at Ellis Island

Filing into an enormous inspection hall, the immigrants formed long lines separated by iron railings that made the hall look like a great maze.

Now the examinations began. First the immigrants were examined by two doctors of the United States Health Service. One doctor looked for physical and mental abnormalities. When a case aroused suspicion, the immigrant received a chalk mark on the right shoulder for further inspection: L for lameness, H for heart, X for mental defects, and so on.

The second doctor watched for contagious and infectious diseases. He looked especially for infections of the scalp and at the eyelids for symptoms of trachoma, a blinding disease. Since trachoma caused more than half of all medical detentions, this doctor was greatly feared. He stood directly in the immigrant's path. With a swift movement, he would grab the immigrant's eyelid, pull it up, and peer beneath it. If all was well, the immigrant was passed on.

The eye examination

Those who failed to get past both doctors had to undergo a more thorough medical exam. The others moved on to the registration clerk, who questioned them with the aid of an interpreter: What is your name? Your nationality? Your occupation? Can you read and write? Have you ever been in prison? How much money do you have with you? Where are you going?

Some immigrants were so flustered that they could not answer. They were allowed to sit and rest and try again.

About one immigrant out of every five or six was detained for additional examinations or questioning.

Often the father came first and sent for his family later. (photo by Augustus F. Sherman)

The writer Angelo Pellegrini has recalled his own family's detention at Ellis Island:

We lived there for three days—Mother and we five children, the youngest of whom was three years old. Because of the rigorous physical examination that we had to submit to, particularly of the eyes, there was this terrible anxiety that one of us might be rejected. And if one of us was, what would the rest of the family do? My sister was indeed momentarily rejected; she had been so ill and had cried so much that her eyes were absolutely bloodshot, and Mother was told, "Well, we can't let her in." But fortunately, Mother was an indomitable spirit and finally made them understand that if her child had a few hours' rest and a little bite to eat she would be all right. In the end we did get through.

Most immigrants passed through Ellis Island in about one day. Carrying all their worldly possessions, they left the examination hall and waited on the dock for the ferry that would take them to Manhattan, a mile away. Some of them still faced long journeys overland before they reached their final destination. Others would head directly for the teeming immigrant neighborhoods of New York City.

Waiting for the ferry to Manhattan, 1912

At Home

Most turn-of-the-century immigrants settled in America's big cities. The immigrants needed jobs. The cities were growing fast and offered the best chances to find work. By 1910, three out of four people in New York City were immigrants and the children of immigrants. The same thing was true in Boston, Cleveland, Chicago, and Detroit.

Many immigrants could not speak English when they arrived. They knew little about American laws and customs. And so they clustered together, living in ethnic neighborhoods where they could mingle with their countrymen and speak their native languages. Almost every major city had its German and Irish neighborhoods, its Polish, Italian, Jewish, and Greek districts. People from the same village in Europe might wind up living as neighbors on the same street in America.

In most cities, immigrants moved into old, run-down

neighborhoods. As newcomers, struggling to gain a foot-hold in America, they occupied the poorest and most congested districts. New York City absorbed more immigrants than any other city. Manhattan's Lower East Side, where so many immigrants settled, became one of the most densely populated places on earth.

A walk through a crowded immigrant neighborhood was like a visit to the old country. The streets were noisy open-air markets. Pushcarts lined the pavements, offering

Orchard Street on New York City's Lower East Side, 1898
(photo by Byron)

fruit, vegetables, poultry, fish, eggs, soda water, and anything else you could think of—old coats for fifty cents, eyeglasses for thirty-five cents, hats for a quarter, ribbons for a penny. Peddlers hawked their wares in a dozen different dialects. Women wearing kerchiefs and shawls haggled for the best prices. Everyone except the kids seemed to be speaking a foreign language. Looking down upon these streets were the brick tenement buildings, where millions of immigrants began their lives in America.

Bargaining with a pushcart vendor

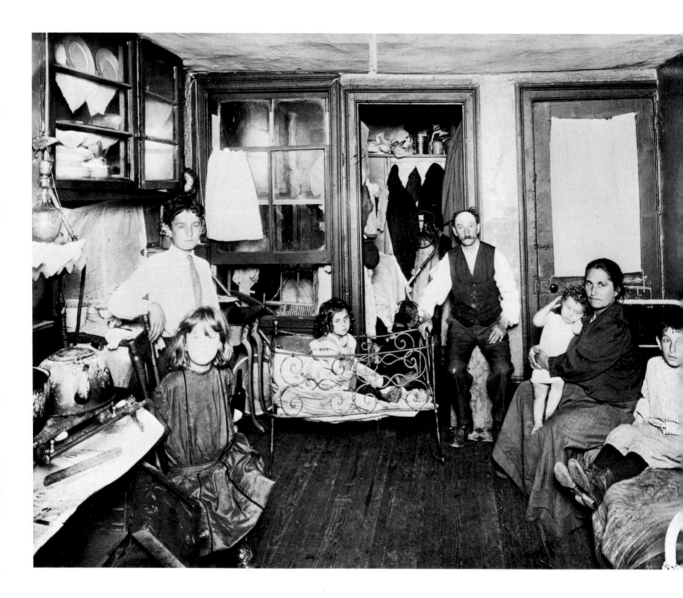

Tenements were jammed with immigrants living in small, cramped apartments. The family shown above used a single makeshift room for cooking and eating, and as a bedroom for the kids. The parents slept in a tiny bedroom to the rear.

A more prosperous family might have three rooms: a

Room in an immigrant family's tenement apartment, 1910 (photo by Jessie Tarbox Beals)

parlor (or living room); a kitchen; and a dark, windowless bedroom in between. The parlor often doubled as an extra bedroom, while the kitchen became the family's social center. In all tenements, the toilet (or water closet) was outside the apartment, in the hallway of the building. It was used by at least two families.

Family supper in a tenement kitchen
(photo by Lewis Hine)

In older tenements, the individual apartments had no running water. Tenants fetched their water from a community faucet in the hallway on each floor. And yet many immigrants had grown up in the old country carrying water from a well. To them, an inside faucet with running water seemed wonderful.

Community water faucet in a tenement hallway
(photo by Lewis Hine)

Leonard Covello has described his family's first American home and his mother's reaction to running water in the hallway:

Our first home in America was a tenement flat near the East River at 112th Street. . . . The sunlight and fresh air of our mountain home in Lucania [southern Italy] were replaced by four walls and people over and under and on all sides of us, until it seemed that humanity from all corners of the world had congregated in this section of New York City. . . .

The cobbled streets. The endless, monotonous rows of tenement buildings that shut out the sky. . . . The clanging of bells and the screeching of sirens as a fire broke out somewhere in the neighborhood. Dank hallways. Long flights of wooden stairs and the toilet in the hall. And the water, which to my mother was one of the great wonders of America—water with just the twist of a handle, and only a few paces from the kitchen. It took her a long time to get used to this luxury. . . .

It was Carmelo Accurso who made ready the tenement flat and arranged the welcoming party with relatives and friends to greet us upon our arrival. During this celebration my mother sat dazed, unable to realize that at last the torment of the trip

was over and that here was America. It was Mrs. Accurso who put her arm comfortingly about my mother's shoulder and led her away from the party and into the hall and showed her the water faucet. "Courage! You will get used to it here. See! Isn't it wonderful how the water comes out?"

Through her tears my mother managed a smile.

Combined bath and laundry in tenement sinks
(photo by Lewis Hine)

In newer tenements, running water came from a convenient faucet above the kitchen sink. This sink was used to wash dishes, clothes, and kids. Water had to be heated on the kitchen stove. Since bathing was difficult at home, most immigrants went regularly to public bath houses.

Tenement apartments had no refrigeration, and supermarkets had not yet been invented. Kids were sent on daily errands to the baker, the fishmonger, the dairyman, or the produce stall. They would rush down rickety tenement stairs, a few pennies clutched tightly in their hands. Since there were no shopping bags or fancy wrappings either, they would carry the bread home in their arms, the herring in a big pan from mother's kitchen.

Carrying home the groceries (photo by Lewis Hine)

Camping out on the fire escape, August, 1916

Many immigrants had to take in roomers or boarders to help pay the rent. Five or six people might sleep in one crowded room. Children were commonly tucked three and four to a bed. Privacy was unknown, and a room of one's own was a luxury beyond reach. When an immigrant family could occupy a three-room apartment without taking in boarders, they were considered a success.

On hot summer days, the stifling tenement rooms became unbearable. Whole families spilled out of their apartments, seeking relief up on the roof or down in the street, where there was some hope of catching a cooling breeze. Kids took over fire escapes and turned them into open-air clubhouses. They put up sleeping tents of sheets and bedspreads, and spent summer nights outside, as elevated trains roared past a few feet away.

Every immigrant neighborhood had its boys' gangs. Rival gangs exchanged challenges and ultimatums. Sometimes they fought pitched battles in the streets—using sticks and stones as weapons, and garbage-can covers as shields.

Each gang ruled its own turf. Members of rival gangs were not welcome, and an unfamiliar face on the street always aroused suspicion. If a boy walked alone through a strange neighborhood, he might be stopped, questioned, and roughed up. If his shortest route to school passed through enemy territory, then he had to take a detour.

Street kids fighting on New York City's Lower East Side (photo by Lewis Hine)

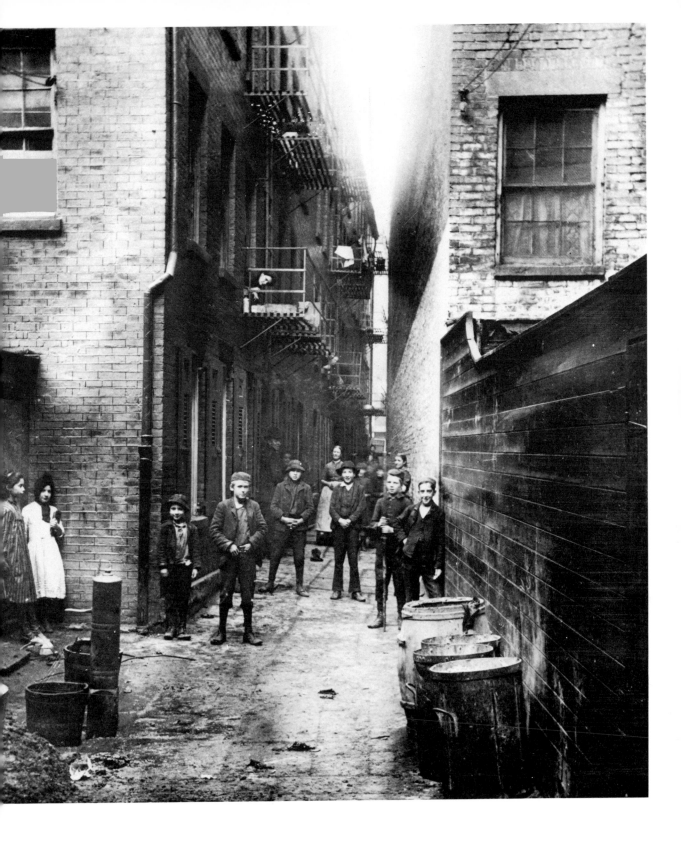

The Mullen's Alley gang, 1889
(photo by Jacob A. Riis)

27

At School

In some city schools, nearly all the students came from immigrant families. When the school term opened in 1903, the pupils of Public School Number 1 on New York City's Lower East Side represented twenty-five different nationalities. Many of these youngsters were fresh from the old country and could not speak English. Students who already knew English acted as translators for those who had just stepped off the boat.

Foreign-born children had to learn how to speak, read, and write a brand-new language. At first there were no special classes for kids who could not speak English. They were simply placed in regular classes with much younger American-born children. A strapping twelve-year-old immigrant boy might find himself squeezed into a desk in a second-grade classroom. As the immigrants learned English, they were promoted to classes with children their age.

This system was unpopular with everyone. It humiliated the immigrant students and slowed down their American-born classmates. Eventually, in most schools with heavy immigrant enrollments, special courses were set up to teach English to newcomers. After four or five months, when the young immigrants had learned enough English, they were assigned to regular classes. Except for those English classes, immigrant children received no special treatment.

Schools had few frills. The school day began with the Pledge of Allegiance. Boys and girls attended separate classes. They came together only in assembly.

The Pledge of Allegiance at the Mott Street Industrial School, New York City, 1890 (photo by Jacob A. Riis)

Instruction emphasized the three Rs, American history and geography, penmanship, and spelling. Misspelled words were written in a notebook ten times or more. Students memorized long lists of names and dates. They recited to the teacher while standing at attention.

Class in New York City's Essex Market School, early 1890s (photo by Jacob A. Riis)

Sophie Ruskay has recalled the grammar school she attended on the Lower East Side:

When teacher called out in her sharp, penetrating voice, "Class!" everyone sat up straight as a ramrod, eyes front, hands clasped rigidly behind one's back. We strived painfully to please her. With a thin smile of approval on her face, her eyes roved over the stiff, rigid figures in front of her.

Beautiful script letters across the huge blackboard and a chart of the alphabet were the sole adornments of the classroom. Every day the current lesson from our speller was meticulously written out on the blackboard by the teacher who, whatever else she lacked, wrote a lovely, regular hand. We spent hours over our copybooks, all conveniently lined, as we laboriously sought to imitate this perfection.

We had to learn our lessons by heart, and we repeated them out loud until we memorized them. Playgrounds were nonexistent, toilets were in the yard, and gymnasiums were an unheard-of luxury.

Some schools had rooftop playgrounds. But usually, there were no sports or play facilities at all. Students stood at their desks as they performed physical fitness exercises every morning. At the command "Class stand!" the room was filled with the shuffling of feet and the banging of desk seats being raised. Monitors used long poles to open the windows. The teacher stood on a little platform beside her desk. She called out, "Breathe in! Breathe out!" as the class made loud hissing sounds. These breathing exercises were followed by simple gymnastics: "Hands on shoulders! Arms up! Arms out! Shoulders back!"

Rooftop playground

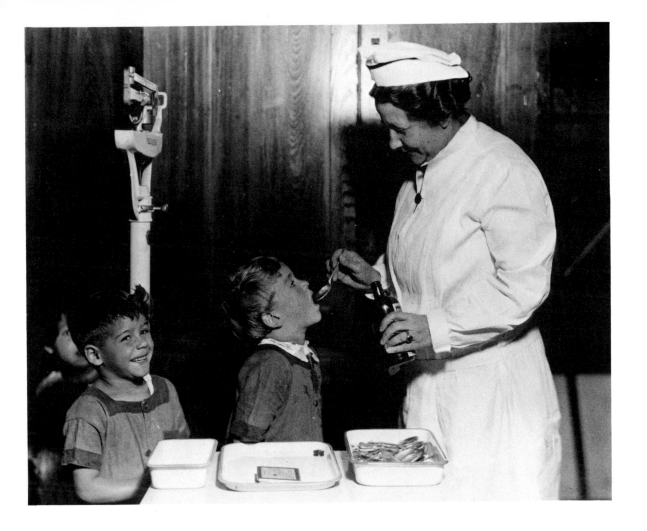

Students were also instructed in the fundamentals of health, hygiene, and personal grooming. Periodic examinations at school by a visiting nurse and visiting dentist provided the only medical and dental care that many children received.

Most immigrant families tried to keep their children in school until the age of fourteen, when a youngster could obtain full-time working papers. But that was not always possible. During hard times, kids had to drop out of school early. In the days before World War I, it was an accomplishment to finish grammar school.

Visiting nurse at a public school
(photo by Lewis Hine)

Practical job training was important. Many kids went directly from grammar school to special vocational schools sponsored by private agencies like the Children's Aid Society in New York City. The society operated separate trade schools for boys and girls. The courses offered reflected the

Boys' printing class

kinds of jobs open to the students. For boys: shoemaking, printing, carpentry, sign painting, bookbinding, basketry, chair caning, janitorial work. For girls: cooking, sewing, embroidery, dressmaking, millinery, stenography, typewriting. Kids who were already working full time could attend

Girls' cooking class (photo by Jacob A. Riis) 35

night classes in English and a variety of other subjects. But after a ten- or twelve-hour working day, it wasn't easy to sit in class and stay alert.

As immigrant kids went through the school system, they were transformed from foreigners into young Americans. They learned about American heroes, American folklore,

Night school (photo by Jacob A. Riis)

and the workings of American government. They absorbed American manners and customs. They became experts on American fads, fashions, and slang. Youngsters entering school often could be identified as little Italians, Greeks, Russians, or Poles. When they left school, they looked, talked, and acted just like other American kids.

Boys and girls attended separate classes but came
together in assembly. (photo by Jacob A. Riis)

At the public library (photo by Lewis Hine)

The children became Americanized much faster than their parents. Often this caused painful conflicts in immigrant families. A gap appeared between the children and their parents. The parents spoke English with heavy accents, if they spoke it at all. They clung to Old World customs and beliefs. The kids spoke English all day with their friends. They thought in American terms. More than anything else, they wanted to be accepted as equals in their adopted land. In their anxiety to become fully "American," some immigrant children rejected their Old World heritage and the traditional values of their parents. They felt embarrassed or even shamed by their parents' immigrant ways.

At Work

Immigrants often had a hard time making a living when they arrived in America. As newcomers, lacking education and skills, they had to compete with each other for the lowest-paying jobs. A man could work twelve or fourteen hours a day and still not earn enough to support his family. Everyone had to help out.

Working children were common everywhere. Kids eight or ten years old worked in factories, warehouses, laundries, and stores. They ran errands, delivered packages, hauled coal and firewood, sold newspapers, shined shoes. Almost everyone over fourteen was employed full time.

Youngsters under fourteen were supposed to be in school, but the law was not strictly enforced.

In 1890, an investigation by the Working Women's Society of New York found that a majority of salesgirls and cashiers in retail stores were under age:

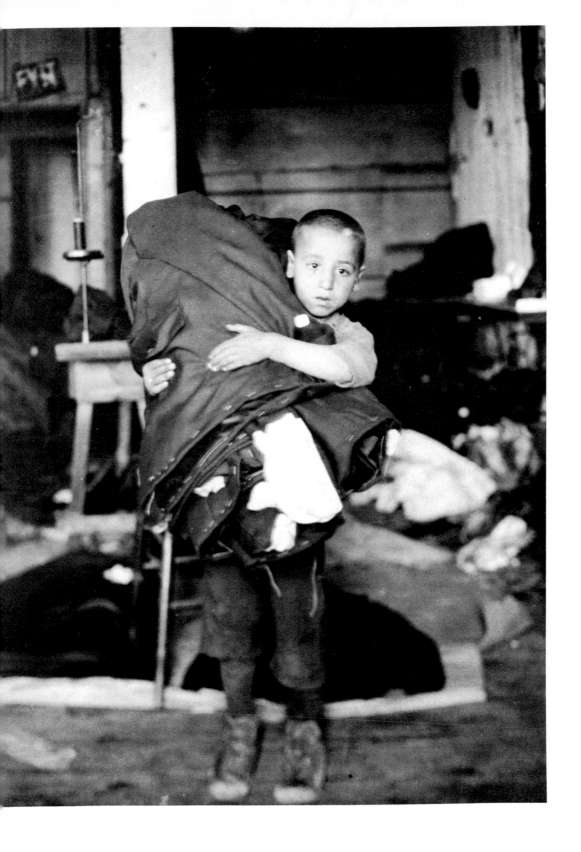

Carrying coats to be sewn at home (photo by Lewis Hine)

The girls are sent to the store before they have fairly entered their teens, because the money they earn there is needed for the support of the family. ...To keep their places they are told to lie about their age and say they are over fourteen....The Women's Investigating Committee found the majority of the children employed in the stores to be under age, but heard only a single instance of the truant officers calling. In that case they came once a year and sent the youngest children home; but in a month's time they were all back in their places and were not again disturbed. When it comes to factories, where hard physical labor is added to the long hours, stifling rooms, and starvation wages, matters are even worse.

In factories, the legal workday was ten hours a day, six days a week. Children under sixteen could not be employed unless they could read and write English. Children under fourteen could not legally be employed at all. But in factories as well as retail stores, the law was often ignored.

Pauline Newman was an immigrant child who worked in a New York City clothing factory:

It was child's work, since we were all children. We had a corner in the factory which was like a kindergarten. The work wasn't difficult. The shirt-waist finished by the [sewing machine] operator

would come to us, so we could cut off the thread
left by the needle of the machine. You had little
scissors because you were children.

Somehow the employer knew when the inspector was coming. Materials came in high wooden
cases, and when the inspector came we were put
into them and covered with shirtwaists. By the
time he arrived, there were no children.

In the busy season, we worked seven days a
week. That's why the sign went up on the freight
elevator: If You Don't Come In On Sunday, Don't
Come In On Monday.

Finishing pants at home (photo by Jacob A. Riis)

Many immigrants worked at home. Tenement apartments became busy workshops where entire families labored seven days a week sewing clothing, making artificial flowers, rolling cigars, shelling nuts for restaurants, and performing other low-paying tasks. Children worked alongside their parents from the time they were old enough to follow directions. Sometimes extra workers were hired, and the apartment became a small factory called a "sweatshop" because of the long hours, hard work, and low pay. It was not unusual to find a dozen or more people—men, women, and children—at work in a stuffy tenement room.

Cigar makers at work in their tenement apartment
(photo by Jacob A. Riis)

45

The journalist Jacob A. Riis described a sweatshop district on the Lower East Side:

Men stagger along the sidewalk groaning under heavy burdens of unsewn garments, or enormous black bags stuffed full of finished coats and trousers. Let us follow one to his home and see how Sunday passes in a Ludlow Street tenement.

Up two flights of dark stairs, three, four, with new smells of cabbage, of onions, of frying fish, on every landing...to the door that opens to admit the bundle and the man. A sweatshop, this, in a small way. Five men and a woman, two young girls, not fifteen, and a boy who says unasked that he is fifteen, and lies in saying it, are at the machines sewing knickerbockers....The floor is littered ankle-deep with half-sewn garments. In the alcove, on a couch of many dozens of "pants" ready for the finisher, a bare-legged baby with a pinched face is asleep. A fence of piled-up clothing keeps him from rolling off on the floor.

The faces, hands, and arms to the elbows of everyone in the room are black with the color of the cloth
on which they are working. The boy and the woman
alone look up at our entrance. The girls shoot glances,
but at a warning look from the man with the bundle,
they tread their machines more energetically than
ever.

Enterprising children often went into business for themselves. Kids peddled matches, shoelaces, and ribbons from
boxes set up on street corners. Young bootblacks, carrying

Bootblacks (photo by Alice Austen)

homemade shoeshine kits, waited for customers in railroad stations, parks, and busy intersections. Newsboys and an occasional newsgirl were familiar sights on city streets as they displayed the latest headlines and shouted, "Extra! Extra!"

Newsgirl and newsboy in front of New York City Hall, 1896 (photo by Alice Austen)

These "newsies" were independent business people. They paid cash for each armload of papers and took the loss for any papers they couldn't sell. They gathered at newspaper offices in the middle of the night, waiting for the early morning editions to roll off the presses.

At the New York Sun, 3 A.M. Waiting for the morning edition to roll off the presses. (photo by Jacob A. Riis)

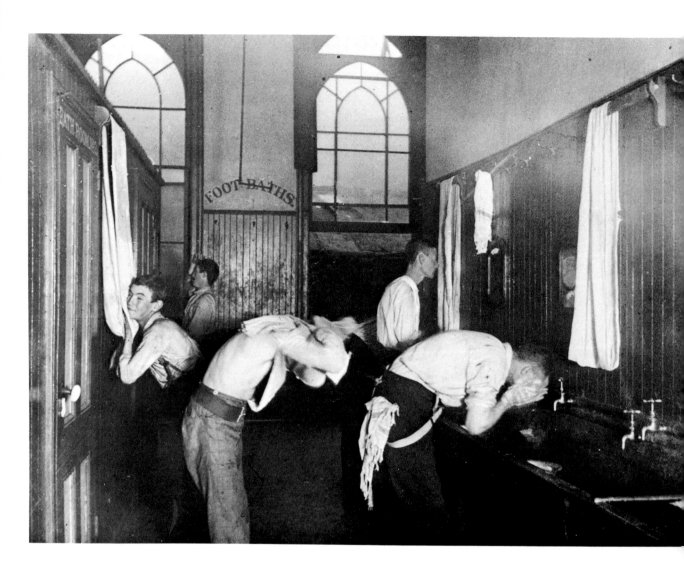

In New York City, thousands of homeless working children—orphans and runaways—lived in lodging houses run by the Children's Aid Society. The society operated five lodging houses for boys and one for girls.

At the huge Duane Street lodging house for newsboys, a resident paid six cents a night for a bunk in the dormitory, six cents for a breakfast of bread and coffee, and six

Getting ready for dinner at the Duane Street lodging house for newsboys (photo by Jacob A. Riis)

cents for a supper of pork and beans—as much as he could eat. Boys were free to come and go as they pleased, but they had to obey the house rules. A notice over the front door read: Boys Who Swear and Chew Tobacco Cannot Sleep Here.

School kids living at home often worked afternoons, evenings, and weekends.

Hauling firewood (photo by Lewis Hine)

Leonard Covello was twelve years old when he took a job delivering bread early in the morning, before school started.

I ran home to tell my mother and father that I had found a job and was ready to do my share in supporting the family. My mother put her hand on my shoulder. My father said, "Good. You are becoming a man now. You have grown up." I was twelve, but I could feel that he was proud of me....

At four-thirty every morning I walked rapidly over to...the bakery shop. There the day's orders were waiting for me to be put into bags for delivery. After a hurried cup of coffee and milk and a couple of rolls, I started out pulling a little wagon that I had constructed out of an old packing crate and baby-carriage wheels....

It was rush, rush, rush, back and forth from the bakery until all the orders were delivered. Then I had to run home and get ready for school. For this work I received one dollar and seventy-five cents a week.

Western Union boy (photo by Jacob A. Riis)

At Play

When kids had free time to meet friends, play games, or just hang out, they took to the streets. Irving Howe has recalled:

> The streets were ours. Everyplace else — home, school, shop — belonged to the grown-ups. But the streets belonged to us. We would roam through the city tasting the delights of freedom, discovering possibilities far beyond the reach of our parents. The streets . . . gave us our first clear idea of what life in America was really going to be like.

Romping through crowded city streets, kids hitched rides on the backs of horse-drawn trolleys, tagged after wandering musicians, and watched cops settle arguments. They listened to fiery soapbox orators and itinerant peddlers of

A cop on the beat settles a dispute,
New York City, 1912. (photo by Lewis Hine)

patent medicines that were guaranteed to cure anything. They chased fire trucks, held secret meetings in alleyways, and pitched coins against buildings.

Almost any game could be played in the streets. No game was more popular than baseball, America's national pastime. Many immigrant kids became baseball fanatics. A detailed knowledge of baseball heroes and statistics was their badge as true Americans.

Baseball in a tenement alley (photo by Lewis Hine)

Where there wasn't enough space for regular baseball games, kids played stickball. The bat—a stick or a broom handle—was used to hit a rubber ball pitched on a bounce. The bases and home plate were marked with chalk on each sidewalk and in the middle of the street. Outfielders were stationed down at the far end of the block. Players spent half their time arguing whether the play had been hampered by passing vehicles and pedestrians.

Correct weight—one cent (photo by Lewis Hine)

Sophie Ruskay has described the different street games played by boys and girls:

Children owned the streets in a way unthinkable to city children of today. There were a few parks, but too distant to be of any use, and so the street was the common playground. The separation of boys and girls so rigidly carried out in the public school also held on the street. Boys played with boys, girls with girls. Occasionally we girls might stand on the sidelines and watch the boys play their games, but our presence was usually ignored. There was no doubt about it, girls were considered inferior creatures. The athletic girl, the girl who would fearlessly decide on a career or even demand the right to study a profession, was still unknown. . . .

We girls played only girls' games. Tagging after us sometimes were our little brothers and sisters whom we were supposed to mind, but that was no great hardship. We would toss them our beanbags, little cloth containers filled with cherry pits. . . . Then we would proceed to our game of potsy. Mama didn't like me to play potsy. She thought it "disgraceful" to mark up our sidewalk with chalk for our lines and boxes. Besides, hopping on one foot and pushing the thick piece of tin, I managed to wear out a pair of shoes in a few weeks! I obeyed her wishes in my own way, by playing farther down the street and marking up somebody else's sidewalk.

Neither my friends nor I played much with dolls. Since families generally had at least one baby on hand, we girls had plenty of opportunity to shower upon the baby brothers or sisters the tenderness and love that would otherwise have been diverted to dolls. Besides, dolls were expensive.

Minding the baby (photo by Jacob A. Riis)

One event that attracted boys and girls alike was the
appearance of the organ grinder, a wandering street musician who carried a heavy hand organ, called a "hurdy-
gurdy." As the organ grinder turned a crank, his hurdy-
gurdy plunked out the cheerful melody of a European folk
song. Some organ grinders traveled with a monkey on a
leash. The monkey rode on the musician's shoulder, wearing an embroidered coat and a miniature bellhop's cap.
When a crowd gathered, the monkey jumped down to the

A hurdy-gurdy man

sidewalk where he collected pennies with one hand while tipping his cap with the other.

Another popular figure was the soda vendor. He traveled from street to street with a gleaming metal container strapped to his back, selling sweet, cool soda by the glass. Most of his customers were working adults, who would pause for a moment's refreshment. The admiring kids who followed the vendor around could not usually afford to buy his soda.

A soda vendor (photo by Lewis Hine)

The iceman also showed up regularly. In the days before
modern refrigeration, city families kept perishable foods in
the icebox. A big chunk of ice was placed in an insulated
compartment at the top of the icebox, while food was stored
on the shelves below. When the iceman came down the
street in his horse-drawn wagon, kids were sent by their
mothers to meet him. They waited while he used a sharp
handsaw to cut a chunk of ice off a huge frozen block.
Then a kid would stoop over, grab the cold, slippery chunk

An iceman (photo by Lewis Hine)

with both hands, lift it from the sidewalk, and lug it up four or five flights of stairs to mother in the kitchen.

On hot summer days, the iceman was the most popular person around. Kids would crowd around him, begging for cold slivers to suck on or to rub across their sweating faces. Sometimes the sanitation man would show up to turn on water hydrants and flush out the gutters. Then kids could kick off their shoes and dance and shout in the fiercely gushing water.

Water gushes from an open fire hydrant on Hester Street, New York City, 1890.

A few children went to summer camps sponsored by the Children's Aid Society and other public service agencies. But most kids spent their summers in the city, working when they had to, playing when they could. For them, a visit to a nearby amusement park was a big event.

There was always something to do. An imaginative youngster could simply stand at a window and play tricks on the people down below.

Hudsonbank Amusement Park, New York City, 1899
(photo by Byron)

64

Samuel Chotzinoff was an immigrant boy who grew up in a tenement apartment overlooking the big fountain in Rutgers Square, a busy New York City intersection:

Standing unobserved at one's window, one could focus a burning glass on the face of a person resting on the stone bench of the fountain and relish his annoyance and anger as he tried helplessly to locate his tormentor. From the same vantage point, one could let down a weight attached to a long string, conk the head of a passerby, and draw up the missile before the victim could look around for the offender; or, with the aid of an accomplice stationed at the curb, stretch a string head-high across the sidewalk, which, unseen by some unsuspecting pedestrian, would lift his straw hat or derby from his head and send it rolling down the street.

Immigrant kids who played street games at the turn of the century grew up to take their places in the daily life of America. They were the first generation in their families to feel truly at home in this country. Today they are old people, those of them who are still alive. They are the great-grandparents of millions of American boys and girls growing up today.

Immigrants still come to America. Since World War II, more than 8 million immigrants have entered the country. While this is a small number compared to the mass migrations at the turn of the century, the United States continues to admit more immigrants than any other nation.

Many of today's immigrants come from countries within the Western Hemisphere, and from Asia and Africa as well as Europe. When they reach the United States, they face many of the same problems and hardships that have always confronted newcomers. And they come here for the same reason that immigrants have always come: to seek a better life for themselves and their children.

An immigrant couple who came to America in 1899
celebrate their fiftieth wedding anniversary in 1931.

Acknowledgments

The idea for this book was suggested by a photographic exhibition called "Street Kids: 1864–1977," held at the New York Historical Society in 1978 to commemorate the 125th anniversary of the Children's Aid Society in New York City. I am grateful to Corbett Jones, who told me about the exhibit and urged me to see it, and to the following people who helped me find the old photographs of immigrant children that appear here: Rita Bunin, Children's Aid Society; Michael Kamins and Martha Jenks, International Museum of Photography at George Eastman House, Rochester, New York; Steven Miller and Esther Blumberg, Museum of the City of New York; Harvey Dixon, American Museum of Immigration, Statue of Liberty National Monument, Liberty Island, New York; and Mitchell Grubler, Staten Island Historical Society.

Russell Freedman,
New York City, 1980

The author gratefully acknowledges permission to quote from the following works:

pages 21–22 and 52, *The Heart Is the Teacher* by Leonard Covello with Guido D'Agostino. Copyright © 1958 by Leonard Covello. McGraw-Hill Book Company. By permission of Blassingame, McCauley & Wood.

pages 31 and 58–59, *Horsecars and Cobblestones* by Sophie Ruskay. Copyright 1948 by Sophie Ruskay. By permission of A. S. Barnes & Company, Inc.

page 54, *World of Our Fathers* by Irving Howe. Copyright © 1976 by Irving Howe. By permission of Harcourt Brace Jovanovich, Inc.

page 65, *A Lost Paradise* by Samuel Chotzinoff. Copyright © 1955 by Samuel Chotzinoff. By permission of Alfred A. Knopf, Inc.

Other quoted works are:

pages 7–8, *In the Shadow of Liberty: The Chronicle of Ellis Island* by Edward Corsi. Copyright 1935 by the Macmillan Company.

pages 13 and 43–44, Thames Television interviews, as reproduced in *Destination America* by Maldwyn A. Jones, Copyright © 1976 by Thames Television, published in the U.S. by Holt, Rinehart & Winston.

pages 42 and 46–47, *How the Other Half Lives* by Jacob A. Riis, 1901 edition, published by Charles Scribner's Sons.

The photographs in this book are from the following sources:

American Museum of Immigration, Statue of Liberty National Monument: frontispiece and pages 3, 9 and 12.

Children's Aid Society: pages 32 and 34.

International Museum of Photography at George Eastman House: pages 19, 20, 22, 23, 26, 33, 38, 41, 43, 51, 55, 56, 57, 61 and 62.

Library of Congress: pages 6, 8, 10, 11, 14 and 17.

Louis N. Freedman: page 67.

Museum of the City of New York: pages 5, 16, 18, 24, 27, 29, 30, 35, 36, 37, 44, 45, 49, 50, 53, 59, 60, 63 and 64.

Staten Island Historical Society: pages 47 and 48.

Index

Italic page numbers refer to captions.